# Men Are Victims Too

Lance D. Williams

Published by Lance D. Williams, 2023.

MEN ARE VICTIMS TOO

**First edition. August 1, 2023.**

Copyright © 2023 Lance D. Williams.

ISBN: 979-8223459163

Written by Lance D. Williams.

# Table of Contents

# Introduction

Since 2014, I've been wanting to focus more on the topics of men being victims of domestic violence, sexual assault, and being falsely accused of these things. I don't feel like it's covered enough. I've seen it so many times over the years, where a man was accused of domestic violence or sexual assault. Their names and characters are raked over the coals for days, weeks, and months. Then it turns out the allegations are false. People and outlets barely spend as much time covering that as much as the original allegations. The person who falsely accused rarely gets raked over the coals or even charged. It's just brushed over, and people move on. I'm not saying all men accused are innocent; that's obviously not always the case. I'm just saying that when it does happen, it should be covered fairly.

I've known for a long time about men getting sexually assaulted, whether in prison, in the military, in frats, or in other ways. It doesn't get as much coverage and support as it does for women. I've always thought it was wrong. Men deserve justice, not judgment, when it happens. People expect men to be tough and not allow those things to happen. When Terry Crews spoke out about being sexually assaulted, I was disappointed to see so many people make fun of him and make light of what had happened to him. People expect the big Black man to be "tough" and knock out anyone who does that to them. Even if he did that after it happened, it still doesn't take away that he was violated and didn't ask for that. Most people would be understanding if it happened to a woman, but with a man, especially the size of Terry Crews, I guess it's hard for people to understand how he could be a victim. There are many stories of teachers having sex with students. The reaction is usually outrage when it's a male teacher and a female student. But when it's a female teacher and a male student, there's not the same outrage, and plenty of men cheer it on, happy for the male student. They don't look at him as a victim. Even if it's consensual in either scenario, it's just interesting to see how people react when it's a different gender. Let's break the stereotypes and focus more on the specific situations and supporting males when they're victims.

Most of the stories in the book have been edited for clarity and to get to the main things they wanted to share.

# Trevor

I had a crazy ex-girlfriend. We used to argue all the time. The cops were called 12 times. I remember one of the times Officer Johnson laughed at me when I told him my girlfriend was beating me up. He said, "Look at you and look at her. You expect me to believe she's beating you up? C'mon man." (Laughing). I tried my best to restrain myself from hitting her back, but it's hard when a person keeps coming at you. I have a right to defend myself at some point. If I didn't let her look through my phone, she would start attacking me.

It takes less than 30 minutes from my job to our apartment. I'm not kidding when I say if I'm not home in 30 minutes after work, she'll flip out on me. She gave me a warning the first time, when I stopped at the store before coming home. The second time I was late, I walked through the door, and she hit me in the face with a frying pan, busting my nose. There was blood everywhere. She said, "I told you, don't be fuckin' late!" I was hurt, I didn't fight back. I was also shocked that she hit me with a frying pan. Ten minutes later, she apologized for hitting me and helped me stop the bleeding. I thought it was a spur-of-the moment reaction, so I let it go.

Another time, she put a knife to my penis and threatened to jam it through. I tried to grab it out of her hand, and during the struggle, she ended up cutting her wrist, and we had to call 911. The paramedics and the cops came. I told them what happened, and they acted like I was the one trying to attack her. I had a conversation with a female neighbor, and my ex saw it. When I came in and drank the Kool-Aid I had on the table, it had a weird taste. I looked at it, and she said, "I let my blood drip in it. Don't disrespect me again." I said, "Disrespect you, how?" She said, "Don't talk to other women around me ever again." I finally understood that she was crazy and that I needed to get out of this relationship. I was convinced she would kill me. When I tried to break up with her, she said she was willing to go to therapy and do couples counseling. She sounded sincere in wanting to make our relationship work, so we stayed together.

In the first few weeks, it seemed like the therapy and counseling were working. We still had arguments, but the physical abuse stopped. One day in counseling, she went off on me and the counselor. She couldn't accept that her issues were the reason for our relationship problems. She said to the counselor, "Fuck you, bitch!" and threw a couch pillow at her. Then she kicked me in the knee. The counselor asked her to calm down. She charged towards her, and I had to grab her before attacking this lady.

The counselor called security, and they asked us to leave. It didn't end there; while we were in the parking lot, we were yelling at each other. A few people called the police when we started pushing each other. I had no more patience; I was tired of holding back and didn't care about getting physical with her. The police showed up and separated us. She said I was smacking her around and she was trying to defend herself, which was a lie. I told them to go ask the counselor and security who the aggressor was. They looked at the parking lot security video and didn't see any evidence of her claims.

I left her there and drove away. So, she had to get an Uber. I went to our apartment and started packing my stuff. I was done with her and ready to move out. Both of our names were on the lease. If I couldn't break it, I would pay half of it. I didn't care about the extra expenses; I just wanted to get away from her by any means necessary. I was putting stuff in my car when she got home, and she started pulling stuff out and throwing it on the ground, telling me I'm not leaving and that I'm a coward for running away. She smacked me in the face. I balled up my fist but held back from hitting her. I tried to call 911, and she grabbed my phone and threw it; when it hit the ground, it broke. She kicked me in the nuts really hard. One of the neighbors said they were calling 911. So, the police showed up again. I told them what happened, and they put her in the back of the police car. They asked me if I wanted to press charges. I said yes, and I want a restraining order too. It was granted.

She still didn't stay away; she came to my job and busted out the windows in my car. The cameras in the parking lot didn't work, so there wasn't proof she did it, but I don't have issues with anybody else, so it's obvious she did it. Just to get away, I quit my job and moved to Pittsburg, California staying with my close friend from college. I finally had some peace when I moved away. I didn't think about men dealing with domestic violence until I went through it with her. I started watching TV shows where men were killed by women, and I thought, 'Damn, that could've been me if I stayed with her.'

# Michael-Allan

I do home repairs. A lot of times, when I go to a home, it's usually the wife at home while the husband is at work. This lady, Lisa, called me and said she had a plumbing emergency that needed to be fixed ASAP. I told her I could be there in 30-45 minutes. When I arrived, she showed me what the issue was. While I was working under the sink, suddenly I heard someone peeing. When I got up from under the sink, there was this young girl naked and peeing; she looked like she was 15 years old. I yelled, "Why would you do that? What's wrong with you?" I storm out yelling for Lisa, and she comes out. I said, "Who the hell is this young chick? She's naked and peeing in front of me!" She said, "That's my stepdaughter Olivia. I'm sure it was just an accident." I said, "How the fuck is it an accident when I'm under sink?" Lisa asked Olivia if it was true. She said, no, she didn't see me. Unless you're blind, there's no way she didn't know I was there. I asked, how old is she? Lisa said she's 17 years old. I said, 'I'm not finishing the job; get someone else to do it.' I was furious.

Lisa said that even if Olivia did that, she's just a young girl probably flirting; it's harmless. I said, "Lady if I did that shit, would you say it's harmless? You would've called the cops so fast!" I went back to the bathroom to get my stuff. Lisa goes to her room to grab her phone to call her husband. While I'm in the bathroom, Olivia comes in and grabs my dick and says, "Why did you tell? We could've had some fun." Then she walks out. Lisa comes in about a minute later and hands me the phone to talk to her husband. I told him what happened, and he also said she probably didn't see me. I didn't even bother telling them about the girl groping me; they'd just make another excuse. I couldn't believe this shit; I'm getting sexually harassed by a 17-year-old girl. I honestly didn't know what to do; if I reported it to the police, they'd either find a way to blame me or not take it seriously. I really didn't even want to tell other people, especially other guys; they'd probably laugh at me. I was wondering if I was overreacting, but I don't think I was. I was 38 years old when this happened; she's 17. My wife said she never even thought about a minor sexually harassing an adult. She said she probably felt bold enough to do it because most grown men would be too embarrassed to admit that it happened and just let it go. That's exactly what I did, because there was no way I was going to be the guy to file a report for that.

# Peter S.

Since I'm blind and disabled, I have caretakers who give me assistance when I need it. I've had a few that have treated me horribly. There was a guy named Jonathan who had very little patience and a bad temper. He would get very physical with me. Sometimes I needed help changing my clothes; he would yank my arms trying to take my shirt off or put it on. He would punch me in the stomach, telling me to stop squirming when he was trying to help me with my shirt. When he tried to pull my pants off, he pulled my legs, yanking me out of my wheelchair, and told me I shouldn't be helpless and do it myself. I don't know for sure, but I think he would put things in my food.

The only time it would taste weird was when he gave me my food. He told me if I ever reported him hitting me, he would come back and get me because it's not like I would see him coming. I believed he would do it and hesitated for a long time to say anything. I finally had to say something when he made my bath water scolding hot and held me back from trying to get out. He claimed it's a legitimate way to help my bones, and he's trying to help me. He was a cruel and evil person, and I didn't want him around me anymore. I reported him to the agency, and they got law enforcement involved.

I had a lady that would come in to help me. She would touch me inappropriately. She rubbed my private parts multiple times. She took my hands and had me touch her breasts, asking me if I liked it. She said blind people are missing out because they can't truly appreciate a naked body. She said we could fulfill each other's needs sexually. She wanted me to stick my fingers in her vagina. I told her I wasn't interested and didn't want to report her, but she needed to stop. She told her agency that I was the one making unwanted sexual advances. This homecare agency didn't care who they hired; I'd rather struggle to take care of myself than have anyone else from there again.

I know other people who are like me: blind, disabled, or both. Some of them have had similar experiences. We're already having a hard time in life, and we're being taken advantage of because of our conditions. It's not right. A nurse told me that, other than kids, we probably have the second-most underreported abuse. The elderly also suffer horrible experiences from people who are supposed to be helping. I don't have any close family members that I can depend on, and I don't trust the agencies to send me someone I feel comfortable with. Without my neighbors, who have been very helpful, I would be stuck struggling on my own.

# Christopher

It has always been my dream since I was 8 years old to join the military and work my way up the ranks while serving my country. In high school, early in my senior year, recruiters came to our school. I went to different tables, looking at the different presentations from every branch. The Marines were always the most appealing to me. When I turned 18, I signed up for the Marines. I went to the Marine Corps Recruit Depot for basic training. I knew early on that I was going to hate military life, and I made a mistake. I made a commitment, and I was going to honor it. I got through boot camp training; it was the hardest thing I've ever done. After that, I continued infantry training. This was a different type of training group; we were told they were trying something new at a different location. I guess our group was the guinea pigs.

I thought it was supposed to be a brotherhood, but most of the guys seemed to enjoy making each other miserable and proving how tough they are. Guys would fight in the barracks constantly. There was this guy, Brian, who had personal beef with me for no reason. I guess I was his target to prove to the others that he's a tough guy. So, he was always starting shit with me to get me to react, but I wasn't trying to fight with him. There was the unwritten code that if a guy challenged you, you must accept or face retaliation from the entire group. Brian made it known in front of everyone that he was challenging me. That means we must fight for 5 minutes. The loser has to get naked and get hit with high-pressure water for 5 minutes. The water is hard and hurts the skin; you'll be in pain the rest of the day.

I didn't want to fight him, but if I don't do it, I face consequences, and if I lose, I also face consequences. The only option was to beat him. I only had about three good minutes in me, and we're going blow for blow. Then I started to get tired, and he hit me over and over, and I kept falling to the ground. My nose is bleeding, and they're calling me all kinds of names and saying I belong with the women. I lost the fight and did the water pressure punishment. It hurt like hell, and it was embarrassing to stand there naked. I'm thinking, 'This is not what I signed up for.'

After I lost, I was challenged by others. I was considered the weak link in the group. I didn't want to do any more challenges and wanted to report our group. If I snitched and they found out it was me, I would be done for. They already didn't respect me, but at least I was still one of them by participating. I refused to do the next challenge and said I was willing to do something else. Later that night, the group stripped me naked, turned me over, and Brian put a stick in my asshole. They said that since I walk around like I have a stick up my butt, I might as well have one in there. It hurt, and I was trying not to cry. If I reported them, everyone would know I did, so I didn't do anything about it.

I remember watching a movie, and the guy that went to prison wanted to make a statement, so he attacked the biggest guy he could find to show he was not to be messed with and wasn't afraid of anyone. I wanted to make that same statement, so while everyone was sleeping, I went over to Brian's bunk, pulled him out of bed, and started wailing on him. I kicked him in the balls so hard that he was yelling in pain. The others woke up and start cheering on the fight. A couple of them said they didn't think I had it in me to do that. Brian was pissed and said I could only beat him while he was sleeping, saying it was a bitch move. I agree; it probably was a bitch move on my part. I was expecting retaliation from him, so I had to stay alert. I didn't really have friends there to have my back, but Brian did. So, Brian and a couple of his buddies jumped me. They held me down, and Brian started fucking me doggy style. He said, "I fuck my bitches from behind, and I'm making you, my bitch." I couldn't move, and they were laughing at me struggling.

I had enough after that. I was tired of fighting and being violated by Brian. I reported him and didn't care that they knew it. I was hoping they would send me home so I wouldn't have to deal with the group anymore. There was only one more week of our training, and the leaders were going to do an evaluation of this group to see if their new training experiment was a success.

They were not satisfied with the results after I reported Brian and learned about our unruly behavior, so they ended the training a week early. There was a justice hearing. Brian and the others had to serve a punishment for their roles in my sexual assault. Brian doesn't deserve to be in the military, he is a psycho. He said he couldn't wait to go over to the Middle East and rape their women and torture their men. Our group was dismissed, and only a few were able to continue to train where it usually takes place. I wasn't a full military member, and my experience was hell. I hated every moment of it.

# Nick

When I went to college, I wanted to join a fraternity. I thought the brotherhood and the networking that comes with it would be really cool. Beta Theta Pi is the organization I wanted to be a part of. The pledge process wasn't as bad as I thought it would be. I've heard stories about pledging and negative experiences with hazing. When I became a member of the fraternity, I loved it. There was a party at a frat house, and I went with several of my frat brothers. Most of us were drinking a lot. We played a lot of drinking games. I passed out.

When I woke up, I was naked. I had stuff on my body: piss, cum, spit, and chips. I was grossed out. I looked around for my clothes and couldn't find them. I walked to the bathroom to get the stuff off me. A couple guys were laughing at me and taking videos of me walking naked. I took a towel from the bathroom to cover myself. When I came out, I asked them, where are my clothes? Dex said someone threw them in the pool. I walked outside, and I saw my shirt floating in the water but nothing else.

There was a girl smoking a cigarette while looking at her phone. She said, "What those guys did to you is fucked up. Never get drunk at a party like this." I wasn't totally sure what they did to me, so I asked her what exactly happened. She said, "You were dared to take off your clothes and helicopter swing your cock. They recorded the video because it wasn't big enough to swing. Then you jumped in the pool. When you passed out, Max pulled out his dick and pissed on you. Mariah was sucking Cade's dick, and he told her to spit the cum on your chest. A few of the guys threw chips and pretzels at you. Everyone was laughing and taking pictures and videos. Nobody tried to wake you up. Sorry, I'm guilty of leaving you hanging too."

I was so embarrassed; it was my own fault for being stupid. The pictures and videos were being sent around. Some people put it on Twitter. While I was talking to her, a guy came out and said, "Little Dick, you woke up." I go back inside, asking my friends to help me find my clothes. They said they were leaving with some chicks; Tate snatches the towel off me and says, "Peace out, little dick." They and the girls started laughing.

The girl I was talking to outside offered to drive me home. I laid my head back and didn't talk much; I was depressed about everything that happened. I didn't want to show my face to anyone again. I didn't know how many people saw the pictures and videos of me naked. I didn't want to be known by the nickname "Little Dick." She tried to cheer me up. She said, "Would it make you feel better if I showed you, my tits?" (Laughing). I laughed and said yes, actually it would. She said, "Of course you're a guy." Then she flashed me.

People were still making fun of me and talking about what I did at the party. A lot of people from our school saw the pictures and videos. I thought I was going to have to transfer schools; I had too much shame. I was invited to more parties, but I said I was never going to go to any more frat parties. I also refused to drink any more alcohol. I wasn't mature enough to handle that stuff. There was a fraternity reception for an event. I went because it was a formal event and not a wild party. I drank some punch, and I set it down. When I left my drink unattended, someone put something in it. I didn't know it until later. So, I finished my drink, and I was feeling strange. I thought I was feeling ill from the oysters I ate. I started feeling lightheaded and having a hard time standing up. I tried to sit down and fell on my ass. Some people started laughing, saying I must be drunk again. I knew I didn't drink this time. I still wasn't aware someone had put something in my drink.

Jonas offered to take me home because I was feeling ill. He said he needed to stop at the frat house to get a box; it'd only take a second. I said, no problem. I guess I dozed off to sleep; it wasn't until I was being smacked with paddles repeatedly that I woke up. I was surrounded by several guys in the yard. I was lying face down, and my pants were down to my ankles. They kept hitting me in the ass with the paddles. I tried to get up, and they kept kicking me down. They said to stay still; it's part of the fraternity ritual. The whacks kept getting harder and harder.

One of the guys put an empty beer bottle between my butt crack and said, we're done. Then they just walked away. Once again, they recorded it. I was so mad. I was looking for Jonas, I felt like he set me up for that to happen. He was gone. I was looking for anyone that I knew; all these guys were random. I couldn't find my phone, so I just started walking. I still didn't feel well, and my head still felt like it was spinning. But I didn't want to be around those guys in case I passed out again. I made it a few blocks, then I collapsed.

A guy walking his dog was trying to help me up. I vomited on his dog; I didn't mean to. He called 911 for assistance. I was trying to tell them in the ambulance what I could recall. They had police officers come and take my statement.

They went to the house to investigate and question the guys. They told the police that I was a known drunk and pill popper, and they tried to help me, but I refused. That was a fuckin' lie. I was done with fraternity life after that. These people weren't my friends. All they tried to do was use me for their entertainment. My reputation on campus was ruined. I dropped out of school because I was so depressed. I rarely wanted to get out of bed or interact with anyone. I went to therapy. I joined a group for males abused in frats. I didn't feel like such a loser, knowing that other guys went through similar experiences. I'm still embarrassed about my past, but warning others not to make the same mistakes I did makes me feel like I have a purpose and not feel sorry for myself.

# Adam

I was a troublemaker growing up. I would break into vehicles and steal from stores; sometimes it was out of necessity. Other times, it was just because I was bored. I spent time in juvenile detention centers; it was like jail but not as bad. When I was 18 years old, I had to spend 30 days in jail. This experience was a lot different than the places I served time as a kid. I was strip-searched, and the guy doing it was a prick; he literally said, "I can make you, my bitch; bend over."

Our cell didn't have any privacy when it came to using the toilet; this guy I was sharing a cell with was staring at me all the time. He would put his hands in his pants. It creeped me out and pissed me off. I had the bottom bunk, and he would stand over me, exposing himself to me. I was an 18-year-old, skinny white kid at the time. This guy was a 32-year-old Black dude built like an NFL linebacker. There's no way I could beat this dude up; I didn't want any issues. I just wanted to do my time and get out.

So, if I had to let him be a creeper, that's the way I was going to let it play out. One of the nights I was sleeping, suddenly I felt something warm hit my face. I woke up, and this dude just shot cum in the face. I hopped up and yelled, "What the fuck, dude!" He pushed me and said, "Keep your voice down, chump." I wiped it off my face and was ready to fight him. He said he would leave me alone if I paid the newbie tax, meaning I had to let something sexual happen, whether it was jerking him off or sucking his dick. I didn't want to do either one, but I decided if I jerked him off, it was "less gay" and it would go by faster. I did it late at night, and he kept his word and left me alone after that.

When I got out, I was asking some of my friends who had been in jail what their experience was like. I was too ashamed to mention what I went through unless they brought it up about their experiences. None of them mentioned anything about being their cellmate's bitch. So, I kept it private. I was really hoping someone would say they had some type of negative experience in that way, so I wouldn't feel alone and like a punk for letting a guy control me against my will.

I hated my jail experience, and it was like a scared straight program for me. I was starting to think twice about committing crimes. Before, I would just do whatever and not care about the consequences. But now, I'm like; 'If this puts me back in jail, it's not worth it.' I just turned 26 years old, and other than a speeding ticket, I haven't done anything wrong. I'm surprised more people don't learn their lessons after being in jail or prison. How can that experience not inspire you to do better? You get no privacy; people are literally looking in your ass. You're getting bossed around all day. Of course, the worst part is being one of the people sexually assaulted, sometimes by inmates and sometimes by the people in charge. I never want to go through that again.

# Ishmael

I'm embarrassed to talk about being abused by my ex-girlfriend. People look at men as the abusers and not the abused. I always think people will think less of me and not consider me masculine if I call myself an abuse victim of a woman. My ex-girlfriend has psychological issues that she won't address. She's bipolar and has extreme anger and rage. When she doesn't get what she wants, she takes it out on other people. When things are going well, she's fine, and that's the person I really enjoy being with.

There was a time I went to the store, and I texted her if she wanted anything. She texted back, "2-liter Pepsi." I bought the 2-liter Pepsi and gave it to her when I got to her apartment. She looked at it and yelled, "You idiot! YOU KNOW I DRINK DIET PEPSI!" Then she hit me in the head with the bottle. I bought what she texted me. I've seen her drink both. I said I could go get her what she wanted, but she'd rather react like a child and have a tantrum. So, she shook up the bottle, opened it, and let it spray on me. Then she dropped it at my feet and left the room, leaving a mess.

She's the type of woman who likes rough sex. It's not really my thing, and I don't enjoy being forceful with my partner. One night, we were having sex, and she wanted me to choke her until she almost blacked out. I didn't want to do that; that's crazy to me. When I refused to do it, she said, "Fine! Just lay back, and I'll give you head instead." I laid back, and then when I was hard, she bit my penis a few times. She said, "Since you won't be rough with me, I'll be rough with you. If I could bite your dick off, I would and give you a pussy, since you are a pussy." If I lost my erection, she would punch me in the face and say I must like men. Because "real men don't get soft being with a woman."

Why I put up with her shit sometimes probably means I have issues too. It finally started to sink in that being with her has no benefit to my life. There are no pros, only cons. I probably should've learned that the first 50 times, but it clicked when I was sitting in my car honking my horn like a crazy person. I was picking her up to go to dinner, but I was 12 minutes late. When she got in the car, I had my right hand on the steering wheel and my left hand looking for the directions to the restaurant. She took handcuffs out and snapped one around my wrist and the other around the steering wheel when I wasn't looking, then got out.

I sat there honking the horn, and people were looking at me like I was crazy. She waited exactly 12 minutes to unlock the handcuffs and said, "You're lucky you weren't 30 minutes late." After that, I knew I had to break up with her, but I'm not going to lie, I was a little afraid to do it. She's not the type to make it easy. I didn't want her to burn up my place like Left Eye did Andre Rison's house. I was watching an episode of *Seinfeld,* and George and Jerry were in the car talking about George breaking up. Jerry said, "Just do it like a Band-Aid. One motion RIGHT OFF!" It felt like a message to me. I had to get it over with. I broke up with her, and I thought she took it well—better than I expected. She was fine with it. She said, "I need a real man anyway." Two months later, she decided to get her revenge for walking away from her. She took dick pictures I had on an old prepaid phone I didn't use anymore that I must've left at her place. She sent them to my grandmother, mom, boss, and almost everyone else on my phone, including my 16-year-old niece.

When I found out, I was so pissed that the rage outweighed the embarrassment. It's the first time I ever thought I might kill her; I was that mad. I couldn't prove she was the one who sent the pictures when I wanted to press charges. It was "technically" a lost phone, so anyone could've done it. I could say that's where I left my phone, but there was no evidence that I did. The lawyer I talked to, and the police basically said, I just have to take this L unless I can prove she did it. The he said, she said was convincing on both sides. I bet if I did that to her, they would take it more seriously. There were so many disrespectful things she did to me during our relationship. I've only told you about a few of them. Nobody should have to deal with abuse, male or female.

# Bryce

My former girlfriend and I didn't have problems until we moved in together. They say you don't really know someone until you live with them. I definitely found that out with her. Everything has to be perfect with her. If I leave a plate in the sink, she'll take it and throw it at my head. If I mess up the bed after she made it, she'll punch me in the face. If she sees crumbs on the floor and I didn't sweep it up, she'll hit me with the broom. I just took it as minor temper tantrums, and I accepted I was the one making the mess.

When I got home after a busy morning, I took a nap on the bed. She came in and held a pillow over my face, because we're not supposed to sleep in the bed until after 8 pm. Those were her rules. I thought it was ridiculous and didn't take it seriously. It's not like we can't remake the bed. I told her she was going overboard with this stuff. She swung her purse at me and hit me in the face, I got a black eye from it. This stuff was in the first month of living together. I was already tired of it. I told her we need to compromise on dos and don'ts living together. It can't just be all her rules. She said if I don't like it, I could get out. So, I said, 'OKAY I'm moving out.' I started packing my stuff and I head down the stairs, she pushed me from behind and I tumbled down the stairs. I broke my wrist.

She's never had this type of anger when we're out in public or when we were at each other's places living separately. I wasn't sure if we should stay together or break up. If we're in this for the long haul, how could we live together if we get married? I talked to her about it, so we could have an idea about our future together, we needed some type of resolution. She said the easy resolution was for me to change and stop being an inconsiderate jackass. She said she brings structure and organization to the relationship, and I just act like I live alone. I understood her point of view. But she didn't seem to think her actions of physical violence were over the top. If someone thinks that's the appropriate way to solve issues, then they don't belong in a relationship, man, or woman. Nobody should be assaulting their partner. I told her, I think it's best we move and go our separate ways. She said I was stubborn for not seeing things her way. I disagree. But she got mad and threw lemonade in my face at the restaurant and stormed off. That confirmed I made the right decision. Her temper tantrums were never going to end, and she was always going to blame the issues on me and take no responsibility for her actions.

# Evan

I met this woman on a dating app. We went on four dates. It was clear we had good chemistry. She said, "I know it might be too soon to do this. But would you be interested in going on vacation with me to Honolulu?" I was down for it, so we went, each paying our own way and splitting the hotel. She asked if I would mind putting the credit card down for the hotel, and she'd make sure she paid her share. I was fine with that. While we were there, the expenses were adding up: expensive meals, wine, and leisure things like spa treatments. She seemed a little upset, like something was on her mind. I asked her, what's wrong? She said her bank is giving her issues for some reason. They put a hold on her account because someone may have gotten ahold of her information, and she wouldn't be able to contribute to our trip and wouldn't be able to pay me back for at least two weeks. She felt bad and was stressed about telling me. I genuinely felt bad and said, 'Don't worry about it; get it to me when you can. Don't let that ruin our trip.' She told me what a great man I was and was blessed to find me.

The third night we were there, we went hard on trying all types of alcoholic drinks. I was drunk, but nothing I haven't been able to handle before. I guess I passed out, and the next morning when I woke up, the room was trashed. I saw Jillian on the floor crying. I ran over to her and touched her. She jumped and got hysterical; her face was bruised up. I asked her what happened. She said, "What do you mean by what happened? You got drunk and whooped my ass because I wouldn't have sex with you!" I don't remember doing that, and it's not in my character to do that, so it was hard for me to believe I was capable of doing that. But I had no reason to doubt her.

My head was pounding. I apologized repeatedly, asking her if there was anything I could do to make up for what I had done. She said that since her account was frozen and she had bills to pay, if I could give her

$3,500 to take care of it and if I promised to never hit her again, she'd forgive me. I agreed to do it.

We planned on staying there for 5 days, but she said she was ready to go after 4 days. I felt bad and wanted to do whatever made her happy. We flew back to our city, and we both went home. The next day, after being back, I went over to Jillian's. She said the medical bills for her injuries were over $400 and wanted me to pay for them. I agreed to do it. I was starting to think, 'Man, being with her has cost me a lot of money.' It wasn't a good sign, and I felt like my spider sense was tingling about her. I still couldn't believe that I was capable of beating her up and trashing the room like she claimed. I thought she might've drugged me. I saw a bill on her table that had a different name than the one that I knew her name to be. When I left, I looked up the name I saw on the table. There were pictures with her mugshots and arrest information. She committed several crimes over the years.

When I confronted her about it, she was angry that I would "snoop around" and look her up. She said I was judging her about her past and deflecting from me whopping her ass to make myself feel better. She said she has pictures of the alleged injuries and even made sure to tell a hotel worker getting ice right after it happened to make sure she had someone to back up her claims.

This bitch had everything planned out and set me up from the beginning. In my short time with her, it cost me over $10,000. My dad told me to just get away from her as fast as possible and don't look back. Trying to fight those claims would cost me more money and more headaches than it's worth. I willingly paid for those things, even if some of it was blackmail. I still wanted to fight it in case she wanted to continue. But I took my dad's advice and moved on. I told her I was done with her. I won't go after her if she doesn't go after me. She was fine with it.

My first experience on a dating app was horrible, and I'll never trust anyone on there again. I'd rather die alone than try to find someone on

Tinder or any other dating app. Being falsely accused and scammed is the worst experience of my life.

# Connor

I used to be addicted to drugs and made a lot of bad decisions when I was on drugs. Picking the wrong partner is what started my downfall. I met this guy, Malik, in high school. He was a star basketball player; he's what you call down-low, a guy that pretends to be heterosexual but likes to have encounters with males. We met by the bleachers near the football field. We were both smoking weed. He asked if I wanted to do ecstasy with him. I had never done it before but was interested in trying. We went to the locker room, and he showed me what to do. It took a while to kick in, but when it did, I really felt it. Malik stripped me naked, bent me over, and started doing me doggy style. I always thought he liked girls. When he was finished, he said if I told anyone about this, he would kill me, and he punched me in the stomach as a warning shot. He punched me so hard that I threw up a little bit.

He and I started doing drugs together often and had sexual interactions. He was really physical during sex and would hurt me often. Sometimes, I would be passed out, and he would have sex with me, and I didn't know it. I had anal problems because he was so forceful. He suffered a serious knee injury in the last game of the season. That stopped colleges from signing him right away. He was angry about it. One night, he had a drug party where everyone just brought whatever pills they had and put them in a bowl. People would grab a handful and just take it, not knowing how bad some of the combinations are. There were a bunch of people who overdosed. A few girls were raped, and I was the only guy that was raped. I heard later three guys took turns on me. Malik told them I was an easy mark. I was hurting so bad from behind that I could barely walk or sit down. I had to go to the hospital.

I went to rehab after that; I blacked out so many times that I lost track. I was taken advantage of so many times that I lost track of that too. I changed my number and tried to avoid Malik. I was walking in the park and Malik and his friends were smoking. He called me over. I tried to pretend like I didn't hear him. So, they ran over to me, and he said, "Don't ever ignore me when I'm talking to you." He put a lit joint on my face. Two of his friends held my arms back, and he punched me repeatedly in the stomach and face. Then he pulls my pants down and exposes me, and he's taking pictures and laughing. They push me down and left.

I thought about reporting it to the police, but I was scared about more retaliation. I was depressed and started taking drugs again. I was miserable and was hoping I would overdose badly enough that it would kill me. I still had anal trauma that required surgery. I took some fentanyl-laced drugs and was slumped over in the car. Someone called 911, and I woke up in the hospital. They were able to save me just in time. I went to rehab again. When I got out, I moved to a different city to get a fresh start. I've been clean for two years now. I heard Malik is in prison. He ruined both of our lives, but at least I've been able to repair mine.

# Jay

There was a woman who is sexual harassment specialist. She came to visit our football team to talk about having boundaries between men and women. In college, sexual interactions happen, sometimes consensual, sometimes forced. Male athletes tend to find themselves in situations where they can get caught up with women and ruin their collegiate opportunities. So, she wanted to give us a seminar to try to avoid those pitfalls. She was a really nice woman and gave a great presentation, which gave us a lot to think about. She was talking with players and coaches afterwards, and she and I had a conversation. She was asking what position I played, what year I was in, where I was from—just basic getting to know me type stuff. When she was about to leave, I offered to help carry her box to her car. She said that would be very helpful. I put the box in the back of the SUV, and she said she'd be here until tomorrow. If I was available for dinner, she'd love to talk to me about an opportunity to be one of her college athlete reps. I said I could do it after 6:30 pm, so we set it up for 7:30. We met at the restaurant, and she was telling me about what the college athlete representative does. I thought it would be a cool opportunity to do it while representing my school and making an impactful difference. We were at the restaurant until about 8:40.

She asked if we would stop at her hotel to get some papers. So, I followed her back and went up with her. She said she's been wanting to tell me all day that she loves my smile and that I would look great on marketing materials. Then she said, "I bet your girlfriend loves your smile." I said, 'I don't have a girlfriend', and she said, "Really!?" I said that football and school take up a lot of my time. She said, she knows how it is, with her traveling she's not able to have a meaningful relationship currently. Then she said, "I know this might seem hypocritical, seeing how I travel to colleges and warn athletes about putting themselves in compromising situations. But I'm really attracted to you. You're not like other athletes I interact with." I was not expecting her to say this to me. My first thought was that this lady is testing me; there's no way she's actually serious. So, I said, "You're good. That's a good test. I'm not falling for that." (Laughing). She said, "I'm serious; I really do like you. I know this is not appropriate, but I don't want to lie about how I feel."

She sat on the edge of the bed and wiped away tears in her eyes, then said, "I can't believe I'm embarrassing myself like this; I'm ruining my credibility." I started to feel bad for her and for some reason felt guilty, so I said, "Look, I do find you attractive too; it was just hard for me to believe you'd be interested in me, especially because of the work you do." I walked over to her to hand her the tissue box. She grabs a couple, then grabs my hand, and looks at me. She said, "I'm sorry for doing this to you; please forgive me." She stands up and we're still staring at each other. She comes closer and then kisses me. I didn't try to stop her, so it was a mutual kiss. She asked me if I wanted to stay a while longer. I said yes. In my mind, I knew everything I was doing was dumb. I'm alone with the lady who just gave a presentation about not doing these things, and I was screwing up hours later.

She and I talked for a while, and I think we both still felt a little uncomfortable about what we were doing. This lady was old enough to be my mom; she's 45 and I'm 21. She's a beautiful woman who looks closer to 25 than 45. We didn't have sex, and other than kissing, nothing else happened. I left around 10:30 p.m. It felt like she wanted me to stay all night, but neither one of us brought it up. We exchanged numbers; she wanted to keep in touch.

Around 2 a.m., she sent a text saying, "I can't stop thinking about you." With a heart emoji. I replied, saying, "I feel the same way." She Facetimed me; I answered, and I heard this vibrating noise. She said, "I'm using this and thinking about you." Then starts moaning. I was turned on. She said, "I'd love to see you masturbate right now." I pulled my boxers down and started doing it. I put the cam where she could watch me, and I was doing it for a while until I busted all over my chest. She said she wished she could lick it up right now. Something about her saying that wanted me to get hard so I could do it again, I was turned on. She said she would love to make this a regular thing we do together. I was down for it.

At least once a week, we would have phone sex. I was hoping we would have real sex eventually. I was really starting to like her. I knew that we could never have a public relationship, but I didn't mind having something private. She said she was having conversations with my coach and administrators at the school about coming back; they wanted to honor her and thank her for helping our team. When she came back, she wanted me to stay at her hotel so we could have sex.

When my coach made the announcement that she was coming back in November, I got excited. One of my teammates said, "That bitch is a fraud." I said, 'Why do you say that?' Knowing he was right. He said, "Man, she talks about setting boundaries and fucking with dudes from every school. She's a hoe." I said, "You know that for sure?" He said, "Hell yeah. You know my cousin, who played for Auburn. She tried fuckin' with him and the former quarterback."

I was thinking, this lady is out of control and bold. I'm thinking she had a thing for me, and she preaches a message she really doesn't believe in. She hit me up a couple days later, and I didn't really want to talk to her. I knew she was hypocritical with me, but knowing this is something she does with lots of people took the attraction away. I told her what my teammate said, she said that was in her old days and that was nothing recent. I told her I wasn't really feeling her anymore. She called me and said she would tell my coach and the school administration about me hitting on her if I ended things. "Who do you think they'll believe, me or you? The last athlete that tried to expose me, I went to his school, and they settled with a big payday. He was kicked off the team. Don't let that be you."

It was my senior year, and I had late-round draft potential. We both had something to lose. If it was true about her reputation, I had the potential to win the dispute. It wasn't worth it for me to go through with it. I told her I would still see her when she came. I went to her hotel. I tried not to think about her blackmailing me into doing this. We had sex; it didn't look like it bothered her at all about what she was doing. I'm not going to lie; while we were doing it, I was enjoying the sex. She's good at hitting the right spots; she keeps you in the mood and makes you want more.

I have a close bond with my position coach, so I decided to tell him about what I did. In case she tried to use it against me in the future, I wanted to get ahead of it, especially during the draft process. He was disappointed that I put myself in a position with the woman who warned us about doing it. He was also pissed off about her using her position to take advantage of athletes. We told my head coach and met with the legal department at the school. There may be a potential lawsuit in the future; things are pending right now. As much as I want to expose her name so people know exactly who she is, I can't do that right now. Some people probably know who I'm talking about. It's not like there's hundreds of women doing this type of work.

When my coach told me that you were looking for men to share their stories about being victims, I wanted to share my experience, so people can learn from my mistakes. I made dumb decisions that could've cost me a lot. It was hard for me to accept that I was a victim and that she's a predator, but it is, what it is. Pretending like it didn't happen doesn't accomplish anything but being open and honest does.

# Todd

My ex-wife would use control to keep me around. After she gave birth to our son, she suffered from medical issues and depression. We were already having issues before she got pregnant; we were the dumb couple that thought having a baby was the solution to keeping our marriage together. It only made it worse. So, after she had our son, her mood would change constantly; sometimes she was extremely sad, or she was extremely angry. I thought about divorce so many times and threatened her that I would leave if she didn't start fixing her shitty attitude. She threatens to take my son and move out of town if we divorce. I have several friends who got divorced and have very little custody and a lot of alimony and child support. I didn't want to end up like them, so the fear of that allowed her to have some power over me. She would also say that when she's really depressed, it's because of me and because I was too hard on her, and I would actually believe it sometimes, so I felt guilty about my role in our arguments.

I was taking a nap on the couch one afternoon when she threw hot coffee in my face, and I woke up yelling in pain. I was disoriented and stumbling around. She then hits me with a baseball bat in my back, then my left leg, and I fall to the floor. She accused me of cheating on her. She was on my laptop and saw that I had a Match.com profile. I admit, I did set up a profile. I never talked to any woman, but looking at profiles gave me some peace. Maybe it's mentally cheating, but I liked reading profiles of potential women, thinking I would be happier with some of the women on there. It gave me something to look forward to if we got divorced. I was in pain for 20 minutes. She smashed my laptop with the baseball bat. After she did that, I was ready for a divorce. I didn't care if she took all my money, and I had no visitation; that's how badly I wanted out.

She called the police and told them I had abused our son. He had all these bruises on his back; I almost cried when I saw them. I knew she did that. I felt so bad for our son; she's the one who would spank him or use a belt on him. I don't believe in hitting kids. Call me soft, but I don't think hurting your kids is the answer. I had been gone all day and had just gotten home, so she had to be the one who did it. She claimed I did it the previous night and that our son just told her about it. I don't know what she did to get him to say I did it, but he backed up her claims.

My theory is that she beat him until he said, I did that to him. Since there was a he said, she said allegation, they wanted to get a social worker involved. She was going to get our son taken away from both of us with her stupid actions. It took a while, but my son finally admitted his mother was the reason for the bruises and not me. I filed for divorce and tried to get an emergency hearing to have custody of my son since she is a danger to him. I left him with my parents while I went to the house to get some things because I was moving out. She wasn't supposed to be at the house, but she came up behind me and hit me on the head with the baseball bat. She kept hitting me and hitting me; it felt like 20–30 times. I was trying to move and grab it, but she was getting some great swings in. She took my phone and left the house.

I was on the floor for at least an hour; I could barely move. I had to crawl to the door; it took all my strength to lift myself up and try to open the door. I made it to the porch but couldn't make it anymore; I was so dizzy. The mailman saw me struggling and ran over to me. He called 911. The ambulance picked me up and took me to the emergency room. I filed a report with the police, and they put a BOLO on my wife. She ditched the car at a shopping plaza. They couldn't find her. Two weeks later, she was found in a different city with a gunshot wound to the head. She had killed herself. We had our issues, and I hated her. But I was sad when I heard she had died. I spent nine years of my life with this woman. I made a human with this woman. There was still some attachment there. I wasn't happy that she died; I just wanted her to get help so we could both live a peaceful life. My son still doesn't understand why his mom is no longer here, and I really don't know why either. I kind of feel responsible for it.

# Peter G.

After I was hired at my job, I would have weekly meetings with the CEO of our company in her office. She would always close the door and lock it, so nobody would walk in. When it first started happening, I didn't think it was a big deal. Nothing wild happened. I did notice a lot of buttons down on her shirt, and sometimes she would bend down over her desk, so her cleavage was showing, and you could see her breasts hanging down, but not the nipples or areola exposed. I was trying not to look; that would be embarrassing if the CEO caught me doing that. She would say that she likes to get to know her staff on a personal level. She would ask questions about our family, relationships, and things we liked to do. She would also share the same.

I told her I was divorced and had a bad experience being married to my ex-wife for 5 years. She said she knows how it is. She went through that with both of her ex-husbands. She said, "I bet the women are all over you, and you have to beat them off with a stick." I laughed and said, 'not really.' She said, that's a shame; they're missing out. I was starting to wonder if she was flirting with me, but I was trying to assume she wasn't. In our third meeting, I asked her about her kids while I was looking at the pictures on her desk. She was telling me about the activities they do and wanted to show me some pictures on her phone. She starts swiping and showing pictures, then ends up showing me a couple nude pictures of her.

She said, "Oh my God, this is so embarrassing; please forgive my inappropriate awkward moment." I said, 'It's okay.' Then she says that since she got personal with me, maybe I would be willing to do the same; that way we'd be even, and she wouldn't feel as awkward anymore. I hesitated. I wasn't expecting my boss to say that to me. I felt bad that I saw her nude, and she was probably embarrassed, so I figured if this would help her not feel as bad, I'd do it. I showed her a naked picture I took in the locker room. She said, "Wow, you have a great body. Thank you for sharing." I felt so weird doing it. I also thought that with the Me Too movement, either I'm a victim of it now or this might come back to bite me in the ass because men get blamed and it's "believe women."

She said, "I don't normally do this with my employees, but would you be willing to have some fun with no strings attached? You won't regret it." Then she sits on my lap, gives me a kiss on the neck, and bits my earlobe. I can't deny it; I liked it and was turned on. I've always had a fantasy about having sex with a hot female boss. She was definitely the type I imagined. I said, "Are you sure you want to do this?" She said, "Absolutely, and I can feel you want to do it too." She felt that I got a boner when she was kissing me. She pulled my pants down and started giving me head. She then took her shirt and bra off, took my hands, and wanted me to start rubbing on her breasts. I couldn't believe I was getting it on with my boss. Her secretary buzzed her intercom, saying an employee wanted to talk to her. She was mad that we had to stop and said she hates interruptions, and we'll finish this later.

When I walked out of her office, her secretary gave me this funny look. I don't know if I was paranoid, but I felt like she knew we were getting it on. I tried not to make eye contact with her. My boss became very demanding of my time. Every time she wanted to have sexual relations, I had to be at her beck and call. It's like she expected me to sit around waiting for her at any moment. I'd be at the gym playing basketball with the fellas, and she'd hit me up. I wouldn't see it until we were done playing, and she'd be like, what took me so long to respond? Her being clingy and demanding was a turn-off for me, and I was less attracted to her.

My sexual performance was getting worse; I wouldn't get hard sometimes or stay hard sometimes. Sometimes, I would cum too fast before we really got going. She said, "Either you're not attracted to me anymore, or you're screwing too many other women. Which one is it?" I said, "I don't know what's going on, but I'm not having sex with anyone but you." She said that if I'm not able to satisfy her anymore, I'm useless to her and that our sexual arrangement is over.

My female best friend and I tell each other everything. I finally told her about the relationship with my boss after it was over. She said, I probably don't realize it or care, but I was taken advantage of by my boss and sexually harassed. I didn't start it, but I felt like it was consensual. I never said no. The more I've thought about it since it happened, the more I know that if I did that, I would be labeled a predator and sexual harasser, and she would be a victim of my actions. But I don't want to look at myself as a victim; I can't shake the gender stereotype. It makes me feel like a lesser man when I look at it that way. So, I convinced myself that what I did with my boss was awesome.

# Lucas

I had been with my ex-girlfriend for two years. I thought we knew each other well. We've talked about most of our lives since we've been together. As it turns out, there was a lot I didn't know about her. I didn't know she was a recovering alcoholic. I didn't know she lost custody of her two daughters because she almost killed them after drinking and driving multiple times. I didn't know she beat up her mom and stabbed her ex-boyfriend with a knife. She kept her wild past a secret. It wasn't until she started drinking again that I found out about the real her.

We went to a sports bar to watch games and hang out with friends. She always told me she didn't drink because she hated the taste of alcohol, so I believed her. When we were at the bar, she said she wanted to try the drink I had. She took the drink and downed it in three seconds. All of us were like, 'Whoa! Are you sure you don't like alcohol?' (Laughing). She said, order her another one of those. From that point on, she kept on drinking the rest of the night. She had at least 18 drinks; I lost count after that. Of course, she was drunk by the end of the night. Throughout the night, she was loud, picking fights with other women, stumbling into tables, and knocking stuff over. I told her you need to slow down on the drinks; she slapped me in the face and said, "Fuck you, you're not my daddy." I let it go because she was drunk.

We took a Lyft back home after we left the bar. She could barely walk up the stairs to our apartment, so I tried to carry her up, but she wouldn't let me. She said she could do it on her own, but she couldn't hold on and fell down the stairs. She threw her shoes at me and said I made her fall. It took almost 10 minutes, but she finally made it inside. She takes off all her clothes and walks out the door to go back outside. She said streaking would be fun; let's do it. I tried to get her back inside, but she yelled, "Get the fuck off me! Help rape, rape!" I said, "Chill out; that's not funny." She laughs and calls me a pussy, then comes back inside. I'm thinking this is going to be a long night.

I was tired and wanted to go to sleep. She wanted to have sex. I said I didn't have the energy for it right now. She said I wouldn't last long anyway and said she needed to call a real man to handle it. She grabs her phone and starts looking for a guy to call. I said, "You're really going to disrespect me like that?" She said, "We know you're a faggot; that's why you like me putting my finger up your butt. I should tell all your friends."

She was starting to piss me off, and I thought about leaving for the night. I went to the couch to go to sleep. I was out for about an hour, then woke up. I look down, and there's a pile of shit on my chest. She's passed out on the floor, lying in shit and piss. My rage meter was high after she took a shit on me. I wanted to kick her so hard, but I left her lying in her own mess. I went to the bathroom to clean myself off. I couldn't believe how wild she was acting. I was never going to let her drink again. The next morning, she wakes up with a massive headache and doesn't remember what she did the night before. I told her, then she punched me in the chest, mad that I left her laying in her own mess all night. I was mad she took a shit on me.

Her behavior changed more and more after that. Every day, she smelled like alcohol and had erratic behavior. I would ask her if she was drunk, and she would cuss me out and hit me, saying don't ever accuse her of that. She was making dinner one night, and the smoke alarm went off because she burned the food. She yelled at me for not reminding her to check on it, even though she never asked me to. She pulled out a knife, put it up to my neck, and said she would kill me in my sleep. She was a whole different person, and I was ready to get away from her. I'm not going to stay with someone who threatens to kill me.

I told her it's time for her to go to AA meetings; she's out of control. Then she said, "I'm not going back there. Fuck you!" When she said that, that's when I started to learn about her past from her mom. Maybe if she had been honest about her past from the beginning, I would've still been willing to go through the storm with her, even with her wild behavior. But I couldn't trust her anymore. I broke up with her.

She was mad I broke up with her, and she told everyone we knew about my private information. The things I liked during sex, talking about how I couldn't satisfy her and the size of my dick. She posted my social security number on social media. She had my Twitter password and posted videos of me masturbating. I had to press charges against her. She was trying to ruin my life. She has major issues, and I didn't really know the real her.

# Rashaun

I work for a record label, so I travel a lot when some of the artists are on tour. I was at a music video shoot, and one of the models that was going to be in the video was flirtin' with me. Even though I'm married, I didn't reject her advances. This woman was a top-tier 10. It's hard to turn away from someone like that. I got her phone number, and we started texting each other all the time. I followed her on Instagram, and some of the pictures she posted were so sexy. I didn't want my comments to be on her page, so I would text her that I liked it and tell her I'd like some exclusives for my pleasure.

She started sending me thirst-trap stuff. She was asking when I was going to start sending some stuff in return. So, I sent some shirtless pictures. I work out a lot, and ladies' comment on my muscles sometimes. She liked the pictures I sent, and she said she wanted to feel me. I said I could make that happen ASAP. We started sending spicy sexts, and she sent me a video of her twerking naked. I sent a video of me masturbating. She texted back, "I could do work on that dick." I wrote, "Let's make it happen."

My wife asked to use my phone when hers was actin' up. I was trying to make excuses so she couldn't use it. She didn't believe me and said, "Let me see your phone. You must be talking to some hoe." I said, "I don't be trying to look at your phone; don't be trying to look at mine. We've got to trust each other." She starts grabbing for my phone, and I'm holding it in the air so she can't reach it. She walks away mad, but I thought she gave up and it was over with. A few minutes later, she comes back into the room, points her gun at me, and demands the phone. I still said no and told her to stop trippin'. She fired a shot past my head. I charged at her, and she shot me in the leg. The phone drops out of my hand, and she runs over and takes it. She said if I didn't give her the pass code, she would shoot me point blank and have her brothers roll up my dead body and dump it in the ocean. I caved and gave it to her.

She looked through my phone and saw all the things between me and this woman. I got up, trying to get something to wrap this wound, and she shot in my direction again, telling me to sit down while still looking through my phone. She was in a rage when she saw that stuff and fired another shot past my head. She said, "Am I not good enough for you anymore?" Before I could answer, she shot me in the arm. She said she really wanted to put some bullets in my head.

She said if I didn't press charges, she would consider us even. She took me to the emergency room, and we lied about how I got my injuries. We said some teens broke into our home and tried to rob us. Law enforcement wanted to investigate our story. They caught us lying and wanted to charge us with making false statements and obstructing an investigation. The prosecutor was trying to say she was trying to kill me and wanted to charge her for that. We worked out a plea deal, and nothing serious happened. I still loved my wife even though I was fuckin' with this other woman. So, I had her back and wasn't going to let her go down on a case when I was the reason for her meltdown.

After that though, my wife was watching me like a hawk. Even if I looked at another woman, my wife was going to go off on me. We went to the mall, and it's natural to look at a woman's butt. Even women do it; it's not like you can always avoid it. So, this woman with a big butt was in front of us in line. She was wearing pants that were see-through, so you could see her ass. I took some looks. My wife caught me, started going off on me in the store, and threw a shoe box in my face. Everybody in the store was looking at us. I was trying to walk out, but she's still yelling at me.

I went to wait for her in the car. She eventually comes out; I thought she was about to get it in, but she throws a rock at the driver's side window. I drove off and left her at the mall. I wasn't about to deal with that drama at the mall. I texted her that I was sorry, but I had to drive off. When she got home, she calmed down, and we talked it out. I thought everything was cool. A few hours later, she asked to look through my phone. I said, "Again with this shit?" She said, 'If you have nothing to hide, then you'll do it.' I wasn't even talking to anyone this time. I don't like all these random ass checks; I'm a grown man. I was trying to compromise, so I said we could look through it together. That wasn't good enough for her.

I tried to walk out of the house. I wanted to leave for a while. She said, we're not done yet, and I can't leave. She was flipping out again. She's punching me in the face, pushing me, and calling me all types of names. I pushed her out of the way and walked out the door. I was gone for two hours. I go back home, and all my stuff is out in the yard. I was pissed off. I opened the door, and she threw a remote at my head. I started yelling at her and told her to help me pick up my shit in the yard. I grabbed some of my stuff and walked back in. She tosses it back out and says, what am I going to do about it? She was trying to bait me into fighting her. She was still calling me all types of names, then slammed the door and locked me out. A couple minutes later, she unlocked the door, helped me bring my stuff in, and apologized. I thought things were fine after that, but I was wrong again.

When I was sleeping, I started feeling punches in the face. I wake up, and her brothers are punching me. One of them threw me out of bed. I'm trying to wake up a little bit and start fighting back, but they're getting me good. They held me down, and she walked in the room, pulled my boxers down, and put a knife to my dick and threatened to cut it off. One of them kept telling her to do it. She starts stabbing me in the stomach, and they start kicking me in the dick and punching me in the face. They said, I better not cheat on her again. I wasn't letting it slide this time. I pressed charges and had them arrested. I filed for divorce. I had my moments of liking other women, but the shit she did to me was a lot worse.

# Brad

I was at a charity event. I met this woman at the roulette table. She kept looking at me with this big smile on her face. I started talking to her and offered to buy her a drink, which she accepted. We went to different gaming areas together. We were both single and feeling each other. I invited her back to my hotel to hang out. I asked her to stay the night with me. We had sex, and it was the best sex I've ever had. This was the first time I had sex with a random woman I had just met. The next morning, I woke up, and she was gone. I couldn't find my wallet, my watch, or my phone. I called the police from my room phone; they came, and I filed a report. A couple weeks later, she was caught and charged. She has a long criminal record. When she took my wallet, she had my address. It was about six months later, and one night I got home and got in the shower. Someone pulled the curtain back, and I looked over with a surprised look on my face because I live alone. There are two women standing there. One of them was the woman who stole from me; she had a gun pointed in my face. She made me get out of the shower; she said if I tried anything, she was ready to pull the trigger because she had nothing to lose. They didn't even let me dry off, and they tied me up to a chair. She started hitting me in the face with the gun. The other woman starts looking around for anything valuable to take.

I said, "You're really going to rob me again?" She hit me with the gun again and told me to shut up. She looked strung out on drugs and didn't really look like she had a plan for how she wanted this to play out.

The woman she was with said, "He knows who you are; you're going to have to kill him." She's pacing around like she's thinking about it. The other woman was taking a bunch of stuff. Then she walks over to me and starts rubbing on my dick. I was getting aroused even though I was trying not to. They had the ropes tied tight; I could barely move. The one with the gun asked if I had any private stashes somewhere. I said no, and the other woman said he's lying; she found my lockbox with $2,000 in it. She hit me in the face with the gun again. The other woman snatched the gun out of her hand and said she was being too nice. She shot me in the foot and said the next one would be in the head or chest. I was yelling and in pain; it felt like my foot was on fire.

They start to argue with each other. The one who didn't shoot me said someone might've heard the shot and told her don't be stupid. You could tell she was the trigger-happy type and was ready to kill me. She kept telling her I needed to die, or she was going to jail. Then she pointed the gun at her and said, "I should kill you both and take all the shit for myself." She tries to take the gun out of her hand, and she shoots her in the thigh. She goes down, screaming in pain. I kept thinking I was going to die tonight. She is unhinged.

She makes her "friend" crawl over to me and demands that she suck my dick. We're both bleeding and in pain. Then she tells her to bite my dick as hard as she can. She does it, and I'm yelling. She's yelling at her, "Harder! Harder!" I started feeling bad for her; she was crying, and I know she didn't plan for this to go off the rails like this. She shoots me in the shoulder and pulls the trigger, pointing at her, and the gun jams up. She panics, kicks her in the head twice, grabs the stuff, and runs out the door.

She was having trouble moving and was trying to untie me. She's crying, saying she's sorry. I was in so much pain and didn't think I was going to make it; I felt like I was going to pass out. She gets enough strength to find her phone and call 911. There were six police officers there, along with the paramedics. They're taking our statements. They placed her under arrest for her role in it. This woman has robbed me twice; I could've died because of her, yet I felt bad for her and didn't want to press charges. It was out of my control; she had too much of a criminal history for them to ignore. She only knew the first name of the other woman and had only met her a few days earlier when they agreed to rob me together, planning with a mutual friend. All three were going to split what they stole from me. The other woman was never found, and the mutual friend who helped plan the crime was also arrested. I recovered from my injuries but suffer from depression. I continue to blame myself for letting that random woman into my life.

# Xavier

I played junior college football. The coaches on our team encouraged hazing and harassment, especially when we screwed up or were being soft. Coach Brown was the worst. I dropped an easy interception; it would've been a pick-six had I caught it. He grabbed my facemask, jerked my head around, and threw me to the ground. Then he points over to an offensive lineman and says, "You know what to do." That meant that I was going to get it in the locker room. He always wanted the biggest people to put us in our place so we wouldn't mess up again. When we were in the locker room, I took off all my equipment and was about to get into the shower when T.J. grabbed me and tossed me across the locker room. My towel fell off, and he started beating me with it. He hit me several times, before some teammates told him that's enough. Another one of my teammates had three penalties called on him, so three people were stomping on him.

We were watching film breakdowns, and someone was looking on their phone; a coach took it and attached it so we could all see on the screen what was on his phone. He showed our teammates personal pictures and videos. He was masturbating in videos. He had a picture bending over showing his butthole. He showed pictures of his girlfriend naked that she sent him. He went through his search history, showing he watched gay porn recently. He embarrassed the shit out of this guy, and I felt so bad for him. The coach said, "If you disrespect me, I'll disrespect you more." We got the point; none of us even thought about taking our phones into the meeting rooms ever again.

The freshman hazing was over the top. Before you were allowed to get a helmet, you had to do whatever a sophomore "leader" wanted. The coaches didn't set any limits and didn't even want to know what we had to do. It was don't ask, don't tell. If you tried to tell, there would be consequences. Some of the things I had to do were lick the shower floor, sniff all the leader's jock straps, kiss the ass of the quarterback, and run up the bleachers naked after midnight. Those things were tame compared to what someone else had to do. One of the things he had to do was put a dildo in his ass and go in and out with it 32 times because that was his jersey number.

Our team was trash; we lost a lot of games. We had such a toxic culture, and it was clear we weren't a team. Just a bunch of misguided savages that weren't good enough to play or coach at higher levels. I left the team halfway through the second year; I didn't even want to finish things out. I was tired of everyone being a dick to each other. Other players left the team as well. I'm not sure if anyone ever reported what was going on there. I know for a fact that the AD knew. He was there at practice when a player threw up on the field, and the coach made him pick it up with his hands and toss it in a trash bag. Hazing has been going on for decades; I don't think there's anything wrong with minor stuff, like singing in front of the team or washing a car. But it crosses a line, making someone do something sexual or letting teammates physically assault each other. I became a coach to mold players the right way. There are too many bad leaders in our society right now.

# Nolan

There are people who believe hitting a woman is wrong and that you shouldn't do it under any circumstance. This assumption that all men are stronger than women is ridiculous. Do you know how many women are bigger and stronger than men? Do you know how many women are capable of abusing men? I swear, people lack critical thinking. I used to date this woman, who is a professional boxer. She's taller than me, weighs more than me, and I'm not gonna lie, she's stronger than me. That's just the way it is. My ex is bipolar and has other mental issues. When she doesn't take her medications, she gets crazy and temperamental as hell. One of the things she does is hear things you didn't say. So, if you say something like, 'You forgot to mail that letter.' She hears you're a forgetful idiot. Then she snaps and starts beating the shit out of you.

We took a trip to Hydra Island, Greece. When we were on a boat, we were on there for like 5 minutes, then she said, she's ready to get off. It was her idea to get on there. So, I brought that up. She got mad, picked me up, and tossed me in the water. The people on the boat were shocked that she did that. A man and woman confronted her; she was about to throw the woman overboard too. The man grabbed her arm; she dropped the lady, then punched the man in the face. The boat had to go back to land because of the commotion. She got into it with the local authorities. It doesn't matter who you are; she'll confront anyone if she feels you're disrespecting her. I've seen this woman get tased repeatedly, and it didn't even phase her. She's like a female Hulk.

I accidentally drank her juice, and she hung me over the balcony and threatened to drop me. Early on in our relationship, she punched me in the face so hard that she knocked two of my teeth out and split my lip open. Another time I had to walk around with a big knot on my head because she threw her cell phone at my forehead. So, I'm sure people will wonder why I would be with someone like that. Well, when she's taking her medications, she's a decent person. But I also stayed out of fear. I felt like if I broke up with this woman, she was crazy enough to kill me. I'd rather take my chances by staying alive and hoping she continues to take her medications. Then, having her snap because I'm leaving her.

I went golfing with my friends. She came to the golf course, took a club out of my bag, and hit me in the testicles with it. Then she hit me in the body several times. She cracked my ribs. When they tried to stop her, she swung it at them. I don't even know what set her off. She got arrested, and I got a restraining order against her. If I stayed, she was going to kill me eventually. If I leave, she will probably try to kill me eventually. At least if I leave, I have a better shot of staying alive by not being around her. That was the conclusion I came to. This woman is one of the strongest people I've ever seen. I won't publicly say the name, but she had a private boxing match against a former heavyweight champion and knocked him out. One of the best fighters of all time went down against her. So, when people act like women are frail and meek, let her punch you when she's in a rage and see how that works out for you.

# Maurice

The reason I'm sharing my story is because you rarely hear about stuff like this. I didn't meet my dad until I was 16 years old. My mom kicked me out of the house because I was in a gang and kept getting into trouble. I got arrested, and the person who arrested me was my dad, but I didn't know it was him at the time. We didn't find out until he was filling out his report at the station. He sat me in the room and started asking me questions about my mom, then he told me he was almost positive I was his son. My mom was 17 years old when she had me, and my dad was 18 and in the military. They weren't a couple; they just had sex. She told my dad she was getting an abortion, and he was fine with that. They went their separate ways and didn't talk again after that. When she was going to terminate the pregnancy, a lady from the church talked her out of it and said she would help raise me.

So, my mom didn't do it. Ms. Avery died when I was 4 years old, and my mom was on her own. Since my mom told my dad she was getting an abortion, she didn't think it was right to shake him down for money years later. My mom always had a hard time controlling me, and it kept getting worse as I got older. I joined a gang at 9 years old. I was a drug runner, because most people wouldn't expect a 9-year-old to have pounds of weed or bricks of coke in their bookbag. When you're that age, you don't realize how much money you're carrying, whether it's the drugs in the bag or the money in your pocket. Slicky, our gang leader, offered me all the candy I could eat to run the drugs. I was risking my freedom and life for candy. Sometimes he would buy me a jersey or some shoes. When I was 12 years old, I finally realized I needed money and not candy. He couldn't trick me with that shit anymore. Slicky had other kids in the gang beat me up for asking for money instead of candy. After that, I turned on the gang and flipped from being with the crips to joining the bloods. I told them where Slicky kept all his drug spots, and they robbed him.

My new gang gave me $4,000 for my cut. They always made sure I had money and protection. I was making more money than mom, so she couldn't tell me anything. I was the one who kept the lights on and food in the house. She knew I was making money doing illegal stuff. She just said, if I get caught, don't call her. When Slicky shot up our house, chasing me down, she kicked me out. I had money, so all I had to do was offer to pay someone to live with them. This 36-year-old lady, who was broke and needed help with bills, said I could stay with her. She knew I was 15 years old. One of the stipulations for living with her was that I had to have sex with her and her daughter. Her daughter was 19 years old. At 15, of course, I thought that was the best arrangement in the world. Some people call it statutory rape; I called it a good ass time. I lost my virginity at 14, so I had a little bit of experience with sex.

When I got arrested at 16, I told the cop (my dad) that my mom kicked me out, so I couldn't go back there. He said he wasn't releasing me to anyone else. So, I was stuck with him. He got it confirmed that I was his son, and he wanted to take me in. He was married and had a 13-year-old daughter. This dude is as strict as they come. I couldn't do shit. The only thing I could do was go to school and do community service. I was trying to hang out with my gang, and he wasn't having it. My dad worked a lot of hours. His wife was unhappy. I liked my experience with older women, so I was going to shoot my shot with her. I would walk around the house naked just to see her reaction. The moment I saw her looking at my dick, I knew I could get her. When she didn't tell my dad, I asked her why. She said she knew he would break every bone in my body and didn't want that for me. She said I must be looking for attention to do that. I said, 'I like attention from older women.' She asked me if I'd ever been with an older woman, and I said yeah, with the lady I lived with before. My stepmother was so much cooler than my dad. I could tell her anything about my past, and she didn't judge me. She let me drink alcohol with her.

One Saturday, my dad and my half-sister were gone. My stepmother and I got drunk. She said she was ready to give me the attention I was looking for. She started kissing me and taking off my shirt. I started taking off her clothes, and we had sex. I was 17 years old, and she was 37 years old. Anytime they were gone, she and I would get it on. She said my dad hasn't been good at sex in 10 years, and I was giving her what she needed. Most of the time, we used condoms; sometimes I would pull them off. I got careless a couple times and released inside of her. Some of my boys made it all the way, and I got her pregnant. She said she could lie and let my dad believe it was his. Or she could get an abortion. We both agreed that an abortion was better. My dad is an investigator and would do every DNA test possible just to make sure it was his. We didn't want that type of heat.

I was getting bored with my stepmom, but she was still into me. I wanted to start fuckin' younger women, but she didn't take it well and said she would tell my dad I raped her if I didn't continue satisfying her needs.

When I turned 18, I wanted to move out. She told me she was pregnant again. I thought she was lying just to keep me around. She kept the used condoms and had audio of us having sex. She said she could lie about us starting when I was underage and said she would keep it this time and admit the affair now that I'm an adult. If I moved out, I had to agree to have sex with her until I was 20.

She was driving home one night when a drunk driver slammed into her, and she died. They found out she was pregnant. I assumed it was mine, but I don't know for sure. My dad was sad. I started to feel guilty about what I was doing with his wife. My dad had colon cancer and died a few years later. I went to therapy and admitted everything. I knew she was going to say that I was taken advantage of by older women. She said I had a role in it as well, but regardless, I'm a victim. When you're a teenager and you can have sex with older women, you think it's cool, and you don't see anything wrong with it most of the time. I didn't feel like I was forced until I turned 18, then I felt trapped.

I'm getting older and more mature. I accept that I did a lot of bad things growing up. The first smart decision I made in my life was going to therapy. I used to think that was for weak-minded people. It has helped me cope with my past. I don't want young people to think how I grew up was cool. There's a lot of trauma and guilt that comes with it.

# Ahmed

When I was in an immigration holding center, I was separated from my wife and kids. I was told we would be there for at least a month. After a month, I was put in a van, and they drove us to another facility. This place wasn't like the other one; it was dark, cold, and wet, and it smelled like urine and feces. The people in charge didn't have any identification; there were no names on the uniform, and they wouldn't tell us what organization they were associated with. A lady made us take off our clothes, and she took pictures of us naked. I was with eight other men. One of them refused to take off his clothes in front of her. She pulled out a taser and used it on him until he hit the ground. He was shaking, and she kicked him in the face. She asked him, "Are you ready to follow directions?" He said, 'yes.' When all our clothes were off, she walked up to each one of us and groped our private parts. She said, "You Brown people have the ugliest dicks." Then she said, "If you think this is a normal processing center, you are wrong. You are here to work for us. You can't come to the United States without earning it first." That's when I knew that this wasn't a government agency but some type of rogue operation.

Some guys took us to a cage. They didn't give us any clothes. It was freezing in there. The cage had nothing in it; we had to sleep on the concrete floor. All of us were shaking. There were two buckets, one for pee and one for poop. If you had to go, it was in front of everyone, and there was nothing to use to wipe if you went number two. A few hours later, they finally gave us some clothes to put on. They knew some of us didn't eat meat, so they said if you wanted to eat, you had to eat the meat that was against your religion or starve. They took pleasure in torturing us. Some of us had to go to a room where there was a doctor giving us clinical trial drugs and random shots that we had no idea what they were injecting into us. We were their experimental test subjects. Some of the side effects led to some people passing out or having bad reactions. When they weren't forcing us to take pills and shots, we had to work all day, sometimes assembling products, sometimes packing boxes, and sometimes loading trucks. They would hit us for no reason; I had various injuries.

I missed my family and was worried about them. I was hoping they weren't going through the same thing I was going through. I was depressed that I might never see them again. I felt bad that I couldn't protect them; I couldn't even protect myself. I was being assaulted by women. One of the days, a lady in charge said she was willing to release one of us if we fought each other. The winner would be released, and the loser would get a bullet in the back of the head. She asked if there were any volunteers. All of us stayed quiet. She said, 'Fine, I'll pick for you.' She grabbed two guys and demanded they fight each other. Jorge hit Nazar. Nazar really didn't want to fight, so he wasn't even trying. Jorge was kicking and punching him, and he was determined to win so he would be released. Nazar was badly beaten; he was bleeding, and he peed on the floor. The lady said, that was fun. She said, but nobody is going anywhere, and they had to go back in the cage. Jorge felt bad about what he did to Nazar but felt like he had no choice.

Some of the guys were getting weak from not eating. They held out for as long as they could, trying not to eat meat. Eventually, they scarfed down the food. There were some new guys that joined us in the facility; there were now 16 of us. Eight in each cage. One of the men was named Abraham. He said he heard the guys transporting them say that the destination was New Mexico. That was the first time we had some information about where we might be located. I tried to keep track of the days I was there, but after 34 days I started to mix up the count and wasn't sure if I was getting the numbers right. I asked the lady how long we were going to be there, and she hit me on the knee with a baton and said don't ask questions. Jorge was getting angry and said, "This is some bullshit. I won my fight. Release me, bitch!" She whacks him in the face with the baton and tells two of the other guys in charge to hold him down. She pulled Jorge's pants down and rammed the baton into his buttocks; he was yelling in pain. She said, "Now who's the bitch?"

Finally, one day, she gathered us around and said, "Good news, sand niggers and border hoppers. You're going to be released. We don't need you anymore." The van ride leaving the facility felt like I was traveling for a week; the trip was so long. Occasionally, we got out to stretch our legs and relieve ourselves. The cover over our eyes was glued on the whole time; it gave me a headache. When I was forced out of the van, I was in the desert. There was nothing around. I had to walk, and I felt so weak, I needed to eat. I didn't have any shoes; I was walking barefoot. I finally saw some people and asked for help. They told me I was in Arizona. They called the police, and I told them what I had been through. I didn't have a lot of information to give them. My main concern was trying to find my family. I had to go to another facility while they investigated things and figured out what to do with me. It took a while, but they finally had information about my wife and kids; they were in Canada. I was able to be transported and reunite with them after 6 months. I never got information about where I was held or who did it. I was just thankful that I was still alive and able to see my family again. I didn't think it would happen. They were safe the whole time and didn't have to go through the hell I did.

# Shane

Throughout my life, I've had mental health issues. I've been placed in psychiatric wards. I've also been to rehab facilities to detox from drugs. I've been put in a behavioral health hospital. I've been to jail and prison. It feels like most of my life I've been trapped in some type of facility because I can't get it right. I'm always screwing up. Every facility I've been to, I've mouthed off to someone. I'm a natural shit talker. My bark is bigger than my bite. I can't fight, so I get my ass kicked a lot!

When I was in prison, I would get into it with different groups. I talked shit to the skinheads when I wouldn't join them. They wanted to brand me with "WHITE PRIDE, WORLDWIDE!" With a swastika sign. I'm not putting that shit on me. I told them, "I hope the niggas in here kill you." I know I shouldn't say the N-word, but I don't always think before I speak. They would attack me after that; I was beat up several times and cut open. They still tried to brand me, but the C.O. stopped them before it could happen. Some of the Black people heard that I used the N-word and wanted to attack me for it. I didn't want any problems with them; I like Black people more than white people, to be honest. The Mexicans wanted me to pay the commissary fee anytime I walked in the sections they hung out. A couple times I told them, "Fuck you, suck my dick spics." Again, I run my mouth without thinking. So, they would jump me. I was probably beaten up at least 20 times while I was in prison. It was probably deserved most of the time.

When I was in the psychiatric wards, I didn't want to take the medications they were trying to give me. I would cuss them out. Some of the male workers got physical with me and sometimes force it down my throat. I refused to eat one time and knocked the tray out of his hands. The food made a mess on his uniform; he picked up the tray and hit me in the face with it. I took a swing at him, and a couple other guys came over to help him; they took turns hitting me in the stomach. They would inject me with shots that would knock me out, just so they wouldn't have to deal with me.

The rehab facilities were probably the best in terms of not dealing with a lot of violence. We would have group sessions sometimes where men and women talked about whatever was on their minds. I liked this woman, Jennifer, who was in rehab with me. Another guy, Thomas, also liked her. Every time I tried to talk to her, he would come push me out of the way and tell me to stop talking to her. He became a bully, always messing with me. He was able to slip me some medications I wasn't supposed to take, and it made me go crazy. I had to leave the facility and go to the hospital. When I was released from the hospital, I couldn't be in the program I was in anymore. I was really trying to stay clean; I did everything I was supposed to do. That made me angry, and I went back to the facility looking for Thomas. I brought a gun, and I was going to shoot him if I saw him. I didn't care anymore. My life sucked, and no matter what I did, I always ended up in some facility getting messed with. I was tired of it, and I wanted revenge. The guards there were able to wrestle the gun away from me and call the police. So, I was back in jail. I thought about hanging myself in the cell. I didn't want to go back to prison. One of the counselors at the facility vouched for me and said they believed Thomas was the reason for my actions. He helped get me into another program.

He felt like I needed to be in a place where I didn't have to be around a lot of people. This was my last chance. I was placed in a group home with three other people. I had my own private room. The people I stayed with weren't violent, and they barely talked. It was the perfect place. I was finally getting the help I needed without people messing with me and setting me back. I've been drug-free for four years. I haven't had any outbursts talking shit to people. I've had a steady job for a few years now. Life is peaceful when people aren't fucking with me or I'm not being a dick to someone.

# Chuck

My wife and I have been married for 22 years. We didn't really have issues until 2020, during the pandemic. That's when we started arguing more frequently. Being stuck in the house more made her angry. She's a social person and loves to go out and do activities. Dining at restaurants, going to the casino, traveling, and other things. In March, when they originally said most things would shut down for two weeks, she was fine with that. Then they kept extending it, and that's what started pissing her off. She had travel plans throughout 2020, but they kept getting cancelled. Every time she got an email about another cancellation, she'd get mad. She threw a flower vase on the floor that we bought in London in 2018. It was an expensive, rare collector's item. I yelled at her for breaking it, and of all things to break, it shouldn't have been that; it's fuckin' stupid.

So, when I yelled at her, she walked over to my bar area and started throwing my personalized shot glasses on the floor, breaking them. I told her she was acting like a fuckin' baby. She starts throwing glasses and bottles at me. One of them hit my head and cut it open. I go over to the mirror to look at it, and she comes behind me and hits me over the head with a bourbon bottle. I kept asking her, 'What the fuck is your problem?' She said, "Being married to you, this damn pandemic, working from home, everything! I fuckin' hate it!"

In July 2020, she wanted to throw a party in the backyard. I said, keep it below 10 people. Our area was strict on that at the time. She had 26 people at our house. In the kitchen, I asked her what happened to keeping it around 10. She said, "What happened to you being a man? You used to be an Alpha; now you're a Beta." I just walked away. She said don't walk away from her, and she threw a plate at the back of my head, frisbee style. I'll be honest; I was close to walking back over to her and getting ready to break her arm. I was tired of her throwing stuff at my head. I probably would have done it if we didn't have company over.

I left the room. She goes back outside and tries to embarrass me. She said, "I guess 16 of you have to go, because Chuck is a pussy and wants to follow the 10-person rule. I married a pussy!" Some of the people started laughing. I left the house to take the dog for a walk. I stayed gone for two hours. When I got back home, the last guest was leaving. I walked into the house, and she said, "Where the fuck have you been? Spending time with your mistress?" I've never cheated on my wife, so I don't know why she would say that. I told her I needed a break from her for a while. She says, "Speaking of break, how about I break this TV?" Then she knocks it over and lets it fall on the floor, cracking the whole screen. She was pissing me off by breaking all our stuff and costing us money.

She was also starting to drink more. She used to be a casual drinker, but now, a couple times a week, she would get drunk. When she didn't have any more alcoholic drinks, she wanted to drive and get more. I took the keys and wouldn't let her leave. I'm not about to let her drive drunk. She got pissed off and threatened to stab me if I didn't give her the keys back. I dared her to try it. I was ready to put her in her place. I was always nice to walk away and not engage in violence. But my patience reached the end, and if we had to go at it, then so be it.

Maybe she knew I was serious, because she tossed the knife in the sink and walked away. Later that night, I was sleeping, and she threw a cup of bleach in my face, saying, "You think I was really going to let you win the argument?" Then she smacked me in the face. My eyes were burning, so I hopped up and went to the bathroom to rinse them. After I cleaned my eyes as best I could for about 15 minutes, I called 911, and I told them if they don't get her ASAP, I will start smacking my wife around. I was pissed off. I called a friend who lives around the corner to come over. It was around 1 a.m. The police came to talk to us. I told them why I called them and said I don't want to get violent with her, but I'm reaching my breaking point. They said I should leave for the night. My friend took me to the emergency room to get my eyes checked. Then I stayed the night at his house.

I was considering divorce for the first time. I was really starting to hate this woman and couldn't take much more. A few days later, after things calmed down, we had a conversation, and we agreed to go to marriage counseling via Zoom. My wife realized she was the main reason for our disputes. The pandemic changed her life and made her miserable; she didn't know how to handle it, so she let the anger take over. Our counseling was helping, and we didn't have any major disputes for a long time. Our next big debate with each other was in 2021, after vaccines were available. She wanted us to get the shots so we could start doing our normal activities again. I wanted to wait; I didn't trust how fast they created vaccines when it usually takes at least 10 years to figure out what works and what doesn't. She got pissed off and said only idiots would ignore expert recommendations about vaccines. I told her to get the shot; I'm not stopping her. If something happens to her because she took it, or if something happens to me because I didn't. It is what it is; we'll see what happens. She got the shots and the boosters. I still held out. She started to travel again. I went to a few places, but other times I couldn't go because I was unvaccinated.

She was getting frustrated that I continued to hold out and not get the shots. I said that at this point, things are going back to normal, and the requirements are being lifted. She said, that's not the point; a lot of people she knew were dying from COVID-19, and most of them weren't vaccinated. The anger issues were returning. She started yelling at me more and started throwing stuff at me again. One of the times I had to go to the emergency room again. I was getting frustrated and thought about divorce for the second time. We separated for a while. At the end of 2022, I moved back in. Time and space helped. We went on a marriage retreat, and we felt like newlyweds again. We're not arguing anymore; there's no more throwing stuff, no more hitting. I think what helped was life returning to normal; the pandemic took a toll on her, like it did for most of us. She just handled it in the worst way.

**(List of My Books)**

*10 Categories of Trivia*

*200 Mixed Trivia Questions*

*AWARDS AND HONORS TRIVIA*

*Black Trivia Book*

*Colleges and Universities Trivia*

*College Trivia Nights*

*Healthy Habits*

*Health and Medical Trivia*

*I'll Tell You Why I Do It*

*Let's Talk About Women's Basketball*

*Making Sacrifices*

*Men Are Victims Too*

*Men in Sports Trivia*

*Music Trivia Book*

*People in Films and Shows Trivia*

*Real-life Lessons*

*Reflecting on My Interactions with Strangers*

*Religion Trivia*

*Stories of Struggling Fathers, Broken Families, and a Broken System*

*Successful Professional Gamblers*

*The Neighborhood Competition*

*Trivia About Occupations*

*Trivia About Politics*

*True or False: 5 Categories Edition*

*True or False: 2024 Olympics & Paralympics Edition*

*True or False: Organizing & Movements Edition*

*True or False: Powerchair Football & Power Soccer Edition*

*True or False: Video Games & esports Edition*

*Women in College Sports Trivia*

*Women in Sports Trivia*

*Worldwide Locations Trivia*

My Email: LanceCares@gmail.com